BACKYARD WILDLIFE

Wild Turkeys

by Kristin Schuetz

BLASTOFF! READERS

BELLWETHER MEDIA · MINNEAPOLIS, MN

Note to Librarians, Teachers, and Parents:

Blastoff! Readers are carefully developed by literacy experts and combine standards-based content with developmentally appropriate text.

Level 1 provides the most support through repetition of high-frequency words, light text, predictable sentence patterns, and strong visual support.

Level 2 offers early readers a bit more challenge through varied simple sentences, increased text load, and less repetition of high-frequency words.

Level 3 advances early-fluent readers toward fluency through increased text and concept load, less reliance on visuals, longer sentences, and more literary language.

Level 4 builds reading stamina by providing more text per page, increased use of punctuation, greater variation in sentence patterns, and increasingly challenging vocabulary.

Level 5 encourages children to move from "learning to read" to "reading to learn" by providing even more text, varied writing styles, and less familiar topics.

Whichever book is right for your reader, Blastoff! Readers are the perfect books to build confidence and encourage a love of reading that will last a lifetime!

This edition first published in 2014 by Bellwether Media, Inc.

No part of this publication may be reproduced in whole or in part without written permission of the publisher. For information regarding permission, write to Bellwether Media, Inc., Attention: Permissions Department, 5357 Penn Avenue South, Minneapolis, MN 55419.

Library of Congress Cataloging-in-Publication Data

Schuetz, Kristin, author.
    Wild Turkeys / by Kristin Schuetz.
        pages cm. – (Blastoff! Readers. Backyard Wildlife)
    Summary: "Developed by literacy experts for students in kindergarten through grade three, this book introduces wild turkeys to young readers through leveled text and related photos"– Provided by publisher.
    Audience: Ages 5-8.
    Audience: K to grade 3.
    Includes bibliographical references and index.
    ISBN 978-1-60014-972-6 (hardcover : alk. paper)
    1. Wild turkey–Juvenile literature. 2. Turkeys–Juvenile literature. I. Title. II. Series: Blastoff! readers. 1, Backyard wildlife.
    QL696.G27S38 2014
    598.6'45–dc23
                                                                      2014002760

Printed in the United States of America, North Mankato, MN.

Contents

Wild turkeys
are large birds.
They have bumpy
heads and necks.

Wild turkeys live in forests, grasslands, and swamps. They stay near trees.

Wild turkeys gather in **flocks**. These small groups eat, sleep, and move together.

The turkeys **forage** for food during the day. They scratch the ground for nuts, berries, and **insects**.

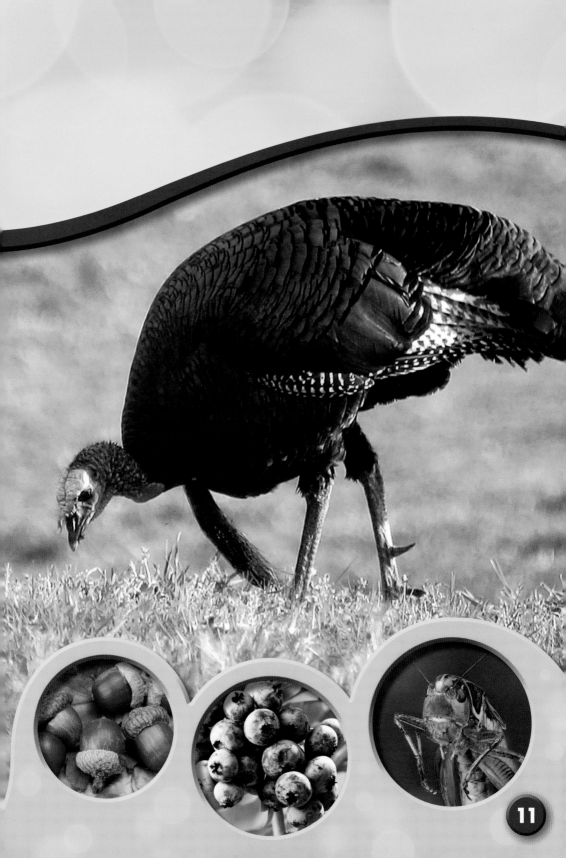

At night they
roost in trees.
There they
are safe from
predators.

Male turkeys are called **toms**. They have bald heads and colorful feathers.

They fan their feathers to impress **hens**. Their heads and necks change color, too.

Then they **strut**. They gobble to attract more attention.

Toms fight one another for hens. They use sharp **spurs** on their legs for battle. She is mine!

spur

Glossary

flocks—groups of wild turkeys that live and travel together

forage—to search for food

hens—female turkeys

insects—small animals with six legs and hard outer bodies; an insect's body is divided into three parts.

predators—animals that hunt other animals for food

roost—to sit or rest in a place, especially at night

spurs—sharp points on the legs of turkeys

strut—to walk proudly

toms—male turkeys

To Learn More

AT THE LIBRARY

Alderfer, Jonathan K. *National Geographic Kids Bird Guide of North America: The Best Birding Book for Kids from National Geographic's Bird Experts*. Washington, D.C.: National Geographic, 2013.

Endres, Hollie J. *Turkeys*. Minneapolis, Minn.: Bellwether Media, 2008.

Magby, Meryl. *Wild Turkeys*. New York, N.Y.: PowerKids Press, 2014.

ON THE WEB

Learning more about wild turkeys is as easy as 1, 2, 3.

1. Go to www.factsurfer.com.

2. Enter "wild turkeys" into the search box.

3. Click the "Surf" button and you will see a list of related web sites.

With factsurfer.com, finding more information is just a click away.

Index

The images in this book are reproduced through the courtesy of: Jeff Banke, front cover; Tom Reichner, p. 5 (top); Bruce MacQueen, pp. 5 (bottom), 9; Minden Pictures/ SuperStock, pp. 7 (top), 21; Aleksey Stemmer, p. 7 (bottom left); majeczka, p. 7 (bottom middle); A and Rob, p. 7 (bottom right); Jeff Kinsey, p. 11 (top); Africa Studio, p. 11 (bottom left); Valentyn Volkov, p. 11 (bottom middle); Sergiy Telesh, p. 11 (bottom right); Patricio Robles Gil/ Sierra Madr/ National Geographic, p. 13; age fotostock/ SuperStock, p. 15; nbiebach, p. 17; westernphotographs, p. 19.